1

MACMILLAN READERS

PRE-INTERM

PATRIC

Kick-off!
The Story of Football

MACMILLAN READERS

PRE-INTERMEDIATE LEVEL

Founding Editor: John Milne

The Macmillan Readers provide a choice of enjoyable reading materials for learners of English. The series is published at six levels – Starter, Beginner, Elementary, Pre-intermediate, Intermediate and Upper.

Level Control
Information, structure and vocabulary are controlled to suit the students' ability at each level.

The number of words at each level:

Starter	about 300 basic words
Beginner	about 600 basic words
Elementary	about 1100 basic words
Pre-intermediate	about 1400 basic words
Intermediate	about 1600 basic words
Upper	about 2200 basic words

Vocabulary
Some difficult words and phrases in this book are important for understanding the story. Some of these words are explained in the story, some are shown in the pictures, and others are marked with a number like this: ...3. Words with a number are explained in the *Glossary* at the end of the book.

Answer Keys
Answer Keys for the *Points for Understanding* and *Exercises* sections can be found at www.macmillanenglish.com/readers.

Audio Download
There is an audio download available to buy for this title. Visit www.macmillanenglish.com/readers for more information.

Contents

A Note About This Story

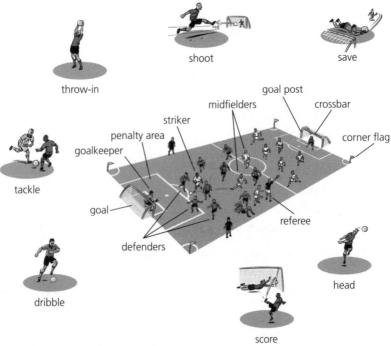

throw-in

shoot

save

goal post

midfielders

crossbar

striker

penalty area

corner flag

goalkeeper

tackle

goal

referee

defenders

head

dribble

score

Football organizations

FA: The *Football Association*, usually known as the FA, is the organization responsible for controlling the rules of football in England.

UEFA: The *Union of European Football Associations* is the organization responsible for controlling football in Europe. It organizes European competitions such as the Champions' League and the UEFA Europa League. The president is Michel Platini.

FIFA: The *Fédération Internationale de Football Association* is the organization responsible for controlling international football. It organizes the World Cup. The president is Sepp Blatter from Switzerland.

4

CONCACAF: The *Confederation of North, Central American and Caribbean Association Football* is the organization responsible for controlling football in these parts of the world.

Football awards

World Player of the Year: This is awarded by FIFA every year.

European Footballer of the Year: This is given to the best player in Europe every year. The player does not have to be from a European country, but they must play in Europe.

Golden Boot: This award is given to the top goalscorer in a competition, including the FIFA World Cup. There are other Golden Boot awards, often called the Golden Shoe, in leagues around Europe as well as the European Golden Boot.

Golden Ball: This is given to the best player at the FIFA World Cup Final. People from the media choose the winner.

Football words

coach someone who trains a sports player or team

reserve a player who has not been chosen to play in a particular match but who is available to play if he or she is needed. The *reserves' team* is the name of the second team of a football club.

substitute a player who replaces another member of his or her team during a sports game

winger one of the players in a game such as football, rugby or hockey who play mainly down the right or left side of the field

linesman someone whose job is to decide whether a ball has gone out of the playing area

free kick in football, an occasion when a player in one team is allowed to kick the ball without any opposition because a player in the other team has broken a rule

hat trick three goals that are scored by the same person in one game

penalty a chance to score a goal in a sports match when the other team has broken a rule

1

Early Ball Games

Ball games have a very long history. Young men and women have been getting together to play them for thousands of years. The earliest games were played in Mexico, South America, at least three thousand years ago. Later games, which had their own rules, were part of the culture of the ancient[1] Olmec and Aztec peoples.

We do not know a lot about these ball games because it is very difficult to understand the written accounts of them. But they were all very similar and in some ways they were like the modern game of football.

The games were played on a special piece of ground – the 'pitch'. The spectators – the men, women and children who watched the game – stood on the terraces and they often bet their gold, slaves[2] and houses on the result of the game. Small figures[3] of the players could be bought by their 'fans'.

In these early ball games, there were two teams of seven players. The players were men who had been captured in wars and kept as prisoners. They played with a ball made of black rubber that probably weighed about five or six kilos. The ball had to be kept in the air – it was not allowed to touch the ground. But the players did not kick the ball. They used their hips, their knees and their arms to keep it in the air and they wore pads[4] to protect themselves.

The players tried to score a 'goal' by getting the ball through one of the two stone rings above the terraces. Perhaps the game ended with this goal, but we are not sure. We know that in some games, the goalscorer was given gold and fine clothes.

How long did the games last? We do not know, but they usually ended in a terrible way, so the players would play for as long as possible. The games were not just about winning a cup, gold or clothes. They were a matter of life and death because they were part of the people's religion. Each game ended in a sacrifice[5] ordered by the priests[6]. When the ball hit the ground, the captain of the losing team would have his head cut off or his heart torn out! Sometimes every player in the losing team was sacrificed. The fans went mad with excitement. The games were followed by a lot of eating and drinking.

These games were still being played in South America when the Spanish arrived in 1519. The soldiers took a team back to Spain, but the game was soon banned[7] there. The Church did not like it.

————

Some Chinese writing, dating from 50 BC, describes football games played between China and Japan. The teams played with a leather ball which was filled with hair. The players could use their backs, chest and shoulders as well as their feet. They could not use their hands. These players must have been very clever. They learnt to do tricks and flicks[8], just like modern players do.

The Japanese game, *kemari*, is also very old and is still played today. The game is not competitive and there are no teams. The players stand in a circle. They pass the ball to each other and must keep it in the air as long as they can.

————

Records show that the Ancient Greeks also played a kind of football from about 2000 BC. There were two teams and the ball could be kicked or thrown. The ball was made from an inflated[9] pig's bladder[10], covered with leather. The Greeks did not have to worry about their kit[11] getting dirty. The players, both men and women, did not wear any clothes at all!

Later, in Italy, in the streets of Rome, boys played a similar game that they called *harpastum*: 'the small ball game'. Roman soldiers enjoyed playing the game too and it kept them fit. The

7

soldiers played on a rectangular pitch, with lines marking the two halves. Only the player with the ball could be tackled. The fans shouted out advice as they do today: 'Too far! Too short! Pass it back!'

A Roman ball game in Rome, Italy, in the second century BC

When the Romans invaded Britain in the first century AD, they played the game there too. We do not know how the players scored goals, but a record[12] of one game tells us that the Roman soldiers won:

England 1– Italy 3 perhaps

2

How Football Began in England

The Romans left England at the beginning of the fifth century AD, but the game of football stayed.

As time went on, the game was played with very few rules and a great number of people. Football was often just an excuse for the young men of one town or village to fight those of another. The players were more likely to kick each other than the ball. This often led to trouble and football became very noisy and dangerous.

In 1314, the mayor of London banned football in his city. The kings of England did not like the game either. They wanted young men to practise archery[13] in their free time. Their bows and arrows were needed in the Hundred Years' War, to kill French soldiers. Football was not useful at all.

By 1555, football was banned in the Universities of Oxford and Cambridge too. Then, in 1581, the headmaster of a big English school thought that he could see some good in football. He believed that with smaller teams, a strict referee and a few rules, the game could become a healthy way of passing the time. And it could teach boys to play together and learn to obey orders.

Nearly one hundred years later, a man called Francis Willoughby wrote the *Book of Sports*. He described the game of football in a way we can recognize today. He wrote about the pitch and the goals – or 'gates' – defended[14] by the best players. The main aim was to get the first goal, and high tackles were not allowed.

———

Young men went on playing football, but there were not many places where they could play because football had been banned from the streets. But rich boys in some big English schools played the game. One of these schools was called Rugby. The school had big fields where lots of boys could play football at the same time.

Then, in 1823, a football player at Rugby School took the ball in his hands and ran with it. And so the game of rugby football – or *rugger* – began. In this game, hard tackles were allowed and several players would fight for the ball. 'Hacking' – kicking the shins of players in the other team – was allowed too.

Other schools, like Charterhouse School, had no fields where they could play rugger. So Charterhouse decided that the ball could not be carried. Kicking people, rather than the ball, was not allowed either.

A few years later, working men, mostly in the north of England, started playing this original form of football. Men who worked in the big factories there wanted to play football with their friends in their free time.

The first football club in the world was started in the northern English city of Sheffield. The club made its own rules – the 'Sheffield Rules'. When other clubs were formed, their rules were different. Soon all the clubs agreed that their teams had to play using the same rules.

In 1863, people from schools and clubs all over England met in a pub in London. They wanted to agree on the rules of football. There were many issues to talk about: should the ball be carried or not? Was hacking allowed? After a lot of talking, the men who wanted to say yes to these questions walked out. They wanted to play rugby football or rugger. The men who stayed decided to work together and so the Football Association[15] was founded.

Over the next few months, the Football Association agreed on fourteen rules. They also agreed on the weight and size of the ball and the size of the pitch.

Only the goalkeeper could touch the ball with his hands. Kicking someone's legs, rather than the ball, was not allowed and players could not trip each other up[16]. They could not use their hands to push or hold their opponents[17] either. Some modern players should remember these last three rules!

Football soon began to be called *soccer* from the word 'association'. The important thing was that the game could now be played in the same way anywhere in the country.

A football game using FA rules, England, in the 1800s

The first game to be played using the Football Association's rules was in 1865. Sheffield FC had a match with Nottingham FC, a club in the English Midlands. During this time, more and more clubs were being formed all over England and Scotland. By 1873, fifty clubs had joined the FA.

These clubs did not have much money. The young men who joined them worked hard at their jobs in factories, offices and shops all week. They played football in their free time and they were not paid for it. They were amateurs – they played for fun and because they enjoyed the game. They played anywhere they could. Their friends came to watch them and everyone had a great time.

———

So the game of football – or soccer – now had rules. The game was beginning to look more and more like modern football, but some things were different.

The goals had no crossbar and no net, just two upright posts. There were corner flags though and corner kicks and goal kicks were already part of the game.

There had been referees since 1840, but the referees shouted at the players because they did not have a whistle. Referees were not given whistles until 1878. They did not have any red or yellow cards in their pocket either. These cards were not used until nearly one hundred years later.

There were other differences too. The ball was made of leather and it was very heavy. All the players in the team wore shirts of the same colour, so that the spectators could recognize them. The players' shirts had no numbers, no names and no sponsors'[18] logos! Their dark leather boots were heavy too. But the teams played a game that we can recognize – it was football!

The football pitch and kit of the late 1800s

3

Football in the Nineteenth and Twentieth Century

In 1888, the world's first football league was founded in England.

This league, known as the First Division, was made up of twelve clubs. These clubs, the best in England, played each other twice every season. Lower leagues were formed in the same way.

Before the end of the nineteenth century, some important changes were made to the game. Goal nets were used for the first time in 1890 and in 1891, penalty kicks were allowed. But it was not until 1905 that the goalkeeper had to stand on his line for them.

By 1894, only one referee was needed for every game, though he had two linesmen – now called assistant referees – to help him.

In 1898, the number of official rules of the game became seventeen. Although some of the rules have changed since then – they were modernized in 1938 and are revised[19] every season – the number is still the same.

Before the First World War (1914–18) all the teams in the First Division played for clubs in the north of England and the Midlands. After the war, some teams from London – Arsenal, Chelsea, Fulham and Tottenham – joined the division.

Soon football was being played in many countries. The game was becoming more and more popular with fans in England and Scotland too. They took it very seriously and they supported their teams every week.

At first, fans could not afford to travel to away matches, but they still watched a game every week. They watched their club's first team one week and its reserves' team the next. As more and more fans went to matches, the big clubs began to build special places – stadiums – where the fans could watch the games being played.

The first stadiums were built where the fans lived, so they were near houses and shops. The fans had to pay to see the games, so walls and gates were built too. At first, other games were sometimes played there, but most stadiums were used just for football.

The clubs wanted as many fans as possible to see their home matches. So wooden terraces were built where people could stand in rows.

At half time, the fans wanted something to eat and drink. So the clubs began to sell food and drink too.

Scotland was slightly ahead of England in building stadiums. Rangers built theirs at Ibrox, Glasgow, in 1887 and Celtic, their close rivals[20], built one in 1892.

1892 was also the year in which the first purpose-built stadium – a stadium built only for playing football – opened in England. It was at Goodison Park, the home of Everton Football Club, in Liverpool. This stadium had high terraces on all four sides of the pitch.

In time, every important club had its own stadium, filled with its own fans. But the 'away fans' – fans who had come to see their team play in a different city – were there too.

Today, only a limited number of fans are allowed to buy tickets when their club is playing away. For Premier League games, this is five per cent of the total number of seats in the stadium and it is fifteen per cent for cup matches.

The away fans must all sit in one part of the stadium. Then they can all cheer and chant[21] together. This arrangement also stops arguments between the two groups of fans.

An early football stadium in England

Up to 1927, only fans watching the matches in the stadiums knew what was happening. Then, on 22nd January of that year, the BBC broadcast the first football commentary[22] on the radio. The match was a 1–1 draw between Arsenal and Sheffield United. FA Cup commentaries followed later that year.

More and more people were becoming interested in football. They were learning to understand the game too, as the commentators described what was happening on the pitch.

There were many great British players in the first half of the twentieth century. It is difficult to compare these players of the past with modern ones. Their kit and the ball they played with were very different. In the past, the ball was made of leather and was very heavy. The modern white ball – with some black, red or another colour on it – is not made of leather, but of a synthetic[23] material[24]. The material is cut into different shapes to form a perfectly round ball. This modern ball is very light, and clever players can make it swerve[25] through the air – or 'bend it like Beckham'. Sometimes, in winter or at evening matches, the ball is yellow, because that colour is easier to see in bad light.

The players' boots were also very heavy in the past. And yet some players were able to dribble the ball a long way. Boots are now much smaller and lighter and they do not cover the players' ankles. These boots help players to run fast and kick cleverly, but they do not protect them very well.

Modern boots are made in many different colours and patterns. The manufacturers[26] pay famous players to wear their boots. Then the fans want to buy them too.

Modern players wear their number and their name on the back of their shirts. But until about 1930, there was only one way the fans could know who each player was – by the position he played on the field.

The teams played in a two-three-five formation[27] and the players did not run all over the pitch as they do today. There were no substitutes, even for injured players.

Players who played in a certain position were always known by the same number. The goalkeeper played in position number one. And, since 1913, he has had to wear a different colour shirt from the other players. Then, the right back was number two etc. The fans could find out each player's name from the programme sold at the match.

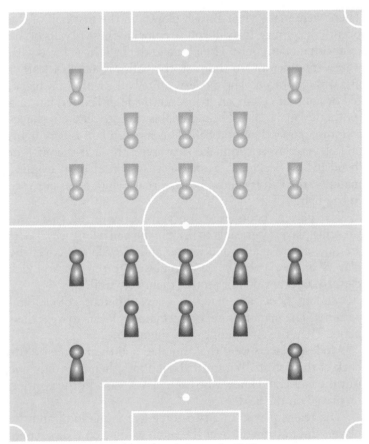

The two-three-five formation of the early 1900s

Then, in August 1928, two London teams played matches in which the players wore their numbers on their shirts. Soon, a few other big clubs began to do the same thing.

The FA did not like the idea and rejected[28] it several times. But in 1939, the FA agreed that numbered shirts could be used. However, that football season was cut short when the Second

World War started and numbered shirts were not worn again until the 1946–7 season.

Famous British players who played in certain positions were known by the number of that position. But if in one match they played in a different position, they wore a different number.

Then, from 1965, substitutes were allowed if a player was injured. These players wore higher numbers. Formations changed too and the old system broke down.

To make things easier, players' names were added to their shirts. Shirts with both names and numbers were first worn in a European match between England and Sweden in 1992. At the end of the 1992–3 season, they were worn by two English clubs, Arsenal and Sheffield Wednesday, in the League Cup Final.

Of course, the fans soon wanted to wear a shirt with their favourite player's name and number on it. The selling of replica[29] shirts quickly became big business.

Great British players of the past

Stanley Matthews must be one of the most famous British players of the past. Born in 1915, Matthews played professional football for thirty-four years. He retired[30] from the game in 1965 – aged fifty!

In all that time, he was never given a red or yellow card. Matthews played for Stoke City – his home club – and also for Blackpool. He was capped – chosen to play for his country – fifty-four times and wore the number seven shirt.

Although he played with the old, heavy ball, Matthews was very quick and he was known as 'the wizard[31] of dribble'. His passing was very accurate[32] too and he made lots of assists[33] for other players.

When the fans knew that Matthews was playing, the stadium was always full! Perhaps his finest match was the Cup

Final of 1953 when he helped his club, Blackpool, win in the final minute.

Matthews was the first football player to be knighted[34], so we should call him *Sir* Stanley Matthews. The great man also won the first European Footballer of the Year Award in 1956.

Sir Stanley Matthews died aged eighty-five in 2000. He was a skilful[35], honest player who never behaved badly on the pitch. People think that he was as good as any British footballer playing today – his manners were certainly better than some of today's players. And he earned only twenty pounds a week!

Alex James, born in 1901, was a Scottish player who had his greatest success with the London club, Arsenal. James made more assists than goals. He had great ball control and was a skilful passer of the ball.

James suffered[36] from many injuries, but he still helped his club to win several awards, including four league titles and two FA Cups.

Dixie Dean is another famous name from the past. Born in 1907, Dean was a striker who played most of his football for Everton Football Club. Like Sir Stanley Matthews, Dean was often tackled very roughly and was injured badly, but he never received a red or yellow card. And in those days, substitutes were not allowed!

Dean was a great goalscorer – he scored thirty-two goals for his club in his first season and sixty in the 1927–8 season. In total, Dixie Dean scored 383 goals for Everton.

He was capped for England sixteen times, scoring eighteen goals – including two hat tricks.

Today, there is a statue of Dixie Dean outside the stadium at Goodison Park, where he played so many great games for Everton.

Cliff Bastin, born in 1912, played in the English schoolboys' match against Wales at the age of fourteen. In May 1929, he signed for Arsenal, who paid the huge fee of two thousand pounds for him. Bastin went on to be the youngest player in an FA Cup Final and later he became the youngest English player to win an England cap.

Bastin played as a quick and clever winger for his club, and as a reliable member of an English side that included the great Sir Stanley Matthews.

Tommy Lawson, born in 1919, was another great Everton player, although he played for several other clubs during his career. Like Dixie Dean, he was a striker and he helped Everton win the league in the 1938–9 season by scoring thirty-four goals.

Bobby Robson, born in 1933, spent many years playing for the London club, Fulham. He also played for England twenty times. Later, he managed both British and European clubs, including Barcelona. He also managed the English national team and led the country to the semi-finals of the 1990 World Cup. In 2002, he was knighted for services to football and became Sir Bobby Robson. Sadly, Robson died in 2009. Important people from the world of football all agreed that this was a terrible loss to the game.

The Charlton brothers, Jack and Bobby, came from a footballing family. Jack Charlton, born in 1935, played for Leeds United as a boy and later as a first team player for more than twenty years. He then managed three English teams and later became manager of the Republic of Ireland team, where he stayed for nine years.

Bobby Charlton, born in 1937, played as both a midfielder and a striker. Most of his career was spent at Manchester United, where he was very successful. Bobby joined the team in 1956 and was part of the young team managed by Matt Busby, known as 'The Busby Babes[37]'.

Two years later, in 1958, the team was on a plane that crashed on take-off at Munich Airport in Germany. More than half of the people on the plane died. Eight of them were Manchester United players. Bobby Charlton survived and, with his brother, was part of the English team that won the World Cup in 1966. He also went on to captain the Manchester United team that won the European Cup, now the Champions' League, in 1968. Manchester United was the first English team to win the competition.

Bobby Charlton was a great player for both his club and his country. Many people think that he was one of the greatest. When he retired from international football in 1970, he had a record number of England caps, but that record has since been broken by Bobby Moore, Peter Shilton and David Beckham.

Duncan Edwards, born in 1936, was a very talented[38] young player, but he died in the Munich air crash. He was twenty-one years old.

Bobby Moore, born in 1941, spent most of his footballing career with the London club, West Ham United. Moore was a defender and he captained his club for ten years. He was also captain of England when it won the World Cup in 1966. Moore won 108 England caps.

Moore's success on the pitch came from good timing and anticipation[39], making him a great player and a great captain. Led by Moore, West Ham won the FA Cup three times and in 1965, the club also won the European Cup Winners' Cup.

But 1966 was Moore's best year. As well as winning the World Cup, he was voted BBC Sports Personality of the Year.

He was then given an OBE[40] by the Queen of England in 1976.

Moore left West Ham in 1974 to play for Fulham. Later, he played for two American clubs before he retired in 1978.

George Best, born in 1946 in Northern Ireland, played his best football with Manchester United. He was with the club for eleven years, from 1963 to 1974. Best was a player of very great skill. He was very fast and able to score with both his right and his left foot.

In 1968, he was part of the Manchester United team that won the European Cup and he was named European Footballer of the Year. His fans said, 'Maradona Good, Pelé Better, George Best.'

George Best was one of the first players who was as famous for his lifestyle[41] as for his skill on the pitch. Many footballers are celebrities now. They sometimes behave badly and are often in the news. Best was like that. His wild lifestyle cut short a great career, but his many fans always loved him.

———

These players came from all parts of Britain, but there is no British football team. England has its own national team and so do Scotland, Wales and Northern Ireland.

All four countries are proud of their own teams and they aim to compete in the international competitions. Scotland, Wales and Northern Ireland also have their own leagues.

The Scottish football clubs have always had loyal[42] fans. All the Scottish Premier League matches are very well attended. The twelve clubs play each other three times in the season.

There is very strong rivalry between certain teams based in the same city. The greatest is between Celtic and Rangers, both Glasgow teams. Religion and politics make matters worse as Celtic fans are Catholics and the Rangers fans are Protestants.

These two teams are the strongest in the league. One or the other of them is usually top of the league at the end of the season and they often win the domestic[43] cups too.

4

Football in Europe

The first international match between England and Scotland took place in 1872 and it ended as a goalless draw. Soon after this, some English clubs started hiring Scottish players to play for them. These men were paid for playing football. They were professional players – football was their job. But some people did not agree with this and there were still many amateur teams playing football.

———

By the middle of the nineteenth century, Britain was a great industrial[44] nation. Clever men had invented[45] new machines and engineers[46] had built them.

Railways were built too and there were soon big factories where many goods could be made quickly and cheaply. These goods were exported to countries all over the world. Young men from Britain went abroad to work and make money. They took the new ideas with them. Many of these men built railways and set up factories in the countries of Europe and South America.

These young men took their footballs with them too, because they enjoyed playing the game in their free time. They soon taught local people to play the game. Football quickly became very popular in the countries of Europe and South America.

———

The first football club in Europe was the Lausanne Football and Cricket Club, founded in Switzerland in 1860. By the end of the nineteenth century, there were football clubs in most of the big cities in Europe.

Soon these clubs joined together to make their country's own football associations. There were several leagues – or groups of clubs – within these FAs. Clubs of the same standard[47] were put in the same league and they played against each other. This made the games fair and more exciting. The best clubs were in the top or first league.

Today, every country has hundreds of teams, but only between twenty and thirty of them are in the top leagues. And only a few players from the top clubs are good enough to play football for their country.

A history of European clubs and players

France

The first football club in France was started in 1863 by some Englishmen who were living and working in Paris. They played their football games in the Bois de Boulogne, an open place in the centre of the city. Fashionable French people stood and watched them. The spectators thought that the game was very strange, but some of the men became interested and wanted to play it too.

A few years later, in 1872, English sailors started another football club in the port of Le Havre. Then Marseille's first club was founded in 1899.

Football had arrived and was soon being played in many French towns and cities. The first football association was set up in 1907. Then, in 1919, it was replaced[48] by the French Football Federation.

The FFF looks after all the football clubs in France. The very best clubs play in *Ligue 1*, France's top league. They include

Auxerre, Marseille, PSG (Paris St-Germain), St-Etienne and Olympique Lyonnais.

Almost from the beginning, France has played an important part in the organization of the game of football. In 1904, FIFA was founded in Paris. FIFA was made up of the associations of eight European countries: Belgium, Denmark, France, Germany, the Netherlands, Spain, Sweden and Switzerland.

By 1925, FIFA had thirty-six members and by 1930, when the first World Cup was played, there were forty-one. Now there are more than two hundred members from all over the world.

Great French players of the past

Michel Platini, one of France's greatest players, was born in 1955. He was a midfielder who could pass the ball very well. He was also very good at taking free kicks, just like David Beckham.

Platini began playing regularly for a club called AS Nancy in 1972 and the club gave him his first professional contract four years later.

Platini first played for his country in the World Cup of 1978. In 1982, he went to play in Italy, where he stayed with Juventus for five years. He scored sixty-eight goals for the Italian club. He later became captain of the French national team. In the European Championship of 1984, held in France, Platini was at his best. He scored nine goals in five games, helping France to win the competition. When he retired at the age of thirty-two, Platini was made the national team coach.

Platini is still an important figure in world football and he has had a lot to say about high wages and the buying of foreign players.

Eric Cantona is another attacking French player. Born in 1966, Cantona began playing for Auxerre, in his country's *Ligue*

Michel Platini playing for France in the European Championship 1984, France

1, in 1983. The striker had a quick temper and he was often in trouble with the French clubs he played for. As a result, he decided to retire in December 1991. But Michel Platini admired Cantona as a player and told him to carry on. So Cantona went to play in England.

After a few months at Leeds United, Cantona was signed by Manchester United. He stayed there for the rest of his career, scored sixty-four goals and was a great success. He became captain of the club in his final year there.

France is now a multicultural[49] society and *Les Bleus*, as the French national team is called, has players from many different backgrounds. One of the most famous and most successful is *Zinedine Zidane*.

This powerful midfielder was born in France, but his parents were Algerian. 'Zizou', as the fans called him, played for clubs in France, Italy and Spain.

His clever passing, courage and knowledge of the game brought him many awards. He was named as FIFA's World Player of the Year three times. He played in the French national team from 1994 to 2006. But his last international game – the final of the 2006 World Cup against Italy – ended badly. Zidane thought that an Italian player had insulted[50] him, so he knocked him down.

Zidane got a red card, but he was also awarded the Golden Ball as the best player in the competition.

Germany

Football was first played in Germany in 1900. SV Hamburg is probably the oldest club in the *Bundesliga*, Germany's top league.

Germany has reached many World Cup Finals and is very successful at international level. German teams always defend well and several of their most successful players have been defenders.

Great German players of the past

Four names stand out from the many powerful players of the past. Two of these players were goalkeepers.

Sepp Maier, born in 1944, was known as 'The Cat'. He was one of Germany's finest goalkeepers and he played in four hundred matches between 1966 and 1979.

Franz Beckenbauer was called 'The Kaiser' – or emperor. He was born in Munich in 1945 and started playing for Bayern Munich aged fourteen. He also played for SV Hamburg and spent some time in the North American Soccer League. He played in three World Cups, losing to England in 1966 and winning in 1974.

Beckenbauer is the only man to have won the World Cup first as a player and then as a manager.

Jürgen Klinsmann was a striker, known as 'The Blond Bomber'. He scored forty-seven international goals. He had a very successful international career and was capped 108 times.

As well as playing for two *Bundesliga* clubs, Klinsmann also played for foreign clubs. These included Inter Milan (Italy) and Tottenham Hotspur (England).

Later, he played for an American club, but he used a different name!

Oliver Kahn, another great German goalkeeper, was born in 1969. He won twelve German awards and three international ones. In 1999, 2001 and 2002 he was named as Best Goalkeeper of the Year.

Italy

Italian footballers have always been known for their clever, graceful[51] style of play.

Modern football was brought to Italy at the end of the nineteenth century. Englishmen took the game to Genoa, but in 1887, an Italian who had worked in England founded a football club in Turin. Since then, the game in Italy has been both very popular and very successful. The national team – *gli Azzurri* or The Blues – has won many competitions.

Some of the most famous teams in the world play in *Serie A*, which is the name of the top Italian league. The *Serie A* teams are based in the big Italian cities. For example, Milan has two teams – AC Milan and Inter Milan. Inter Milan split from AC

Milan in 1908. These teams share the San Siro Stadium, but they are great rivals. So too are Roma and Lazio, the two clubs based in the capital city, Rome.

Turin, in the north of the country, is the home of Juventus. Juventus was founded in 1897 by a group of schoolboys. The name means 'youth'. Juventus soon became the chosen club of many Italian immigrants[52], so it was called 'The Girlfriend of Italy'. In the 1930s, in spite of[53] its name, the club had several rather old players. So Juventus became 'The Old Lady' and is still known by this name today.

The city of Turin has another team too – Torino, the rival of Juventus.

Great Italian players of the past

Paulo Rossi, born in 1956, played as a striker for his national team and for several Italian clubs, including Juventus and AC Milan. Rossi played for Italy in three World Cups and was included in Pelé's list of greatest living footballers.

His best games were played in the World Cup matches of 1982 when he helped Italy to defeat Brazil, Argentina and Germany. Rossi scored three goals against Brazil and another three against Germany in the final. He was awarded the Golden Boot that year, and was also named European and World Footballer of the Year.

Gianfranco Zola was born in Sardinia in 1966. He began playing professionally in 1984 and signed for the Italian team, Napoli, in 1989. There he was able to train with the great Maradona.

Like Maradona, Zola is short – 1.66m – but this did not stop him being a powerful player. He could twist and turn with the ball and put it past the best goalkeepers. He could curl the ball in a free kick too – something he learnt from Maradona.

In 1996, Zola joined the English club, Chelsea, and he

helped them to win several cups. All together, he played 249 games for Chelsea and scored fifty-nine goals. Zola was very popular with the Chelsea fans and they named him their best ever Chelsea player in 2003.

Zola returned to Sardinia, where he played for Cagliari for the last two years of his career. He also played for Italy for several years and later became the national team's coach.

In September 2008, Zola returned to England to manage West Ham and he was soon popular with its fans too.

Roberto Baggio, who was born in 1967, retired in 2004. In that year, he was in Pelé's list of greatest living footballers. Baggio played all his club football in Italy, where he scored goals for several famous teams. They included Juventus, AC Milan and Inter Milan.

In 1993, Baggio was named European Footballer of the Year and FIFA World Player of the Year.

Francesco Totti was born in Rome in 1976 and has spent his whole career with his local club, Roma. This has made him very popular with the Roma fans. Totti, a striker and attacking midfielder, was named as Italian Footballer of the Year in 2000 and 2001.

Totti has suffered from many serious injuries during his career, but he still became his club's best ever goalscorer. In the 2006–7 season, Totti was the top scorer in *Serie* A with twenty-six goals for Roma. He is also the club's most successful captain.

The Netherlands

The first Dutch club was started in Haarlem by the Dutchman, Pim Mulier, in 1879. Soon there were other clubs all over the Netherlands. In 1889, ten clubs joined together to make the Dutch Football Association. In 1904, the association became part of FIFA and the country played its first international game in 1905. In 1907, when the Dutch played England, they wore their now famous orange shirts for the first time. The Netherlands is not a large country and it did not take part in early international contests because it lacked money. However, the country did take part in the Olympics.

Then, much later, in 1974, with the help of Johan Cruyff, the Netherlands gave the world 'total football'. In total football, players changed their positions as the game went on. It was exciting to watch and difficult to play against.

By this time, the most famous Dutch clubs included Ajax, Feyenoord, PSV Eindhoven and FC Twente.

Great Dutch players of the past

Johan Cruyff was perhaps one of the most important Dutch footballers ever. He was born in 1947 and was named European Footballer of the Year three times – in 1971, 1973 and 1974.

Cruyff trained with Ajax from the age of twelve. He played for the first team from 1964 to 1973 as an attacking midfielder and later played in Spain, for FC Barcelona. He then went on to play for teams in America before returning to the Netherlands. He ended his career with Feyenoord. He also played for his country for twelve years – from 1966 to 1978. When Cruyff retired in 1984, he was successful as the manager of Ajax and then Barcelona.

Frank Rijkaard, born in 1962, was both a player and a manager. He began and ended his career at the Dutch club, Ajax. He also played in Portugal and Italy.

Rijkaard joined Ajax aged seventeen and stayed there for seven years. Then he had an argument with the Ajax manager, Johan Cruyff, and left to play for AC Milan. There he was very successful as a midfielder, playing with other Dutch players – Marco van Basten and Ruud Gullit.

After five great seasons in Milan, Rijkaard returned to Ajax in 1993. He stayed there for two years and he helped the club to win the Champions' League. In the final, Ajax beat Rijkaard's old club, AC Milan.

Rijkaard played for his country until 1994 and won seventy-three caps. Later, as a manager, he liked to make his teams play exciting, attacking football. He managed the Dutch national team from 1998 to 2000.

He went on to manage Sparta Rotterdam in the Netherlands and FC Barcelona. In 2006, Rijkaard helped the Spanish team to win the Champions' League.

Ruud Gullit, born in 1962, learnt to play football in the streets of Amsterdam. He played for several Dutch and Italian teams. Towards the end of his career, Gullit joined the English team, Chelsea.

Gullit was a midfielder, but he could play in several positions. He began his professional career with Haarlem in 1979 and in 1982, he moved to Feyenoord, where he played with Johan Cruyff. In 1984, Gullit was named Dutch Footballer of the Year. While playing with PSV Eindhoven, his next club, he was given other awards, including the European Footballer of the Year and World Player of the Year.

Gullit played in sixty-seven matches for PSV Eindhoven. In 1987, Silvio Berlusconi, owner of AC Milan, paid a record fee to bring Gullit to the Italian club. Two other players from the Netherlands were already there – Marco van Basten and Frank Rijkaard. They and several other great Italian players helped the club to win the European Cup, now the Champions' League, in 1989 and 1990.

Gullit also played international football for the Dutch national team until 1993. Then, in that same year, he moved to another Italian club, Sampdoria. Two years later, he went to play for the English team, Chelsea.

Later, Gullit managed several English teams, including Chelsea and Newcastle. He then spent several years working as a football commentator.

Marco van Basten began playing football for a local club in Utrecht at the age of seven! His professional career began in 1981, when he joined the Amsterdam club, Ajax, aged seventeen.

Two years later, van Basten scored his first international goal as a member of the Dutch national team. He went on scoring goals and in 1986, he won the European Golden Boot with thirty-seven goals in twenty-six matches.

After playing 133 games for Ajax, Marco van Basten was signed by AC Milan in 1987. In his first season with Milan, van Basten had a bad ankle injury.

But 1988 was a great year for him internationally. The Netherlands won the European Championship and van Basten was the best goalscorer of the competition. His goal in the final was one of the greatest in the history of football.

Marco van Basten went on playing great football for his club and his country and was given many awards. But in 1995, his career was ended by his old ankle injury. At the end of his last match, he did a lap of honour[54] and seventy thousand supporters cheered the great player for the last time.

Dennis Bergkamp was born in Amsterdam in 1969. He learnt his football through the Ajax youth system, which he joined at the age of twelve. Bergkamp went on to be a successful Ajax player. He played 239 games for the club and scored 122 goals. From 1993 to 1995, the skilful striker played for Inter Milan, but his greatest years were spent at the English club, Arsenal.

Bergkamp soon became a favourite with the English fans and stayed at the London club for eleven years. As second striker, he worked well first with Ian Wright and then with Thierry Henry.

Bergkamp first played for his own country in 1990. He scored many great goals in international matches. He was known as 'The Dutch Master' and 'The Iceman' because of his calm and clever passing.

During his career, Bergkamp helped his clubs and country to win many awards. In 2007, he was given a place in the English Football Hall of Fame.

Portugal

Portugal's oldest professional football team was founded in 1903 and others soon followed. Today, the best-known clubs are FC Porto and Benfica in Lisbon. These and other first-class teams are part of the Portuguese *Liga*.

The national team usually does well in international competitions. It played in a semi-final of the World Cup in 1966 and 2006.

Great Portuguese players of the past

Eusébio da Silva Ferreira was the top scorer for Portugal in the 1966 World Cup. He has been called the greatest Portuguese player of all time. Eusébio was born in Africa, in the Portuguese colony[55] of Mozambique, in 1942. He began playing football there, but went to Portugal in 1961. He was soon signed by the Lisbon club, Benfica.

Called 'The Black Panther', Eusébio was praised[56] for his long runs past defenders and his clever touches on the ball.

During his career, Eusébio was given many awards. He was voted European Footballer of the Year in 1965 and scored nine goals in the 1966 World Cup. He was the first winner of the European Golden Boot in 1968 and won it again in 1973. A knee injury forced Eusébio to retire in 1975.

Luis Figo is another great Portuguese footballer, but he spent most of his career playing for Spanish and Italian clubs. Five seasons were with Barcelona and five with Real Madrid. Born in 1972, Figo first played as a professional in 1989 and he became part of Portugal's 'golden generation'.

In 1995, Figo was signed by Barcelona and went to play in Spain. He helped the club to win the UEFA Cup Winners' Cup and played in 172 matches.

But in 2000, Figo moved to Barcelona's greatest rival – Real Madrid. Figo helped Real Madrid to win many awards. He was the first of the 'galacticos' – or superstars – to be signed by the club. In later seasons, he was not as successful and in 2005, he moved to Inter Milan on a free transfer[57]. Figo did better at the Italian club and became an important member of the team.

He also helped Portugal to reach the final of the 2004 European Championship and in 2006, he took his country to the semi-final of the World Cup as captain of the national team.

Spain

Football is very popular in Spain and games are very well attended by the Spanish fans. Two Spanish clubs – Barcelona and Real Madrid – are among the most famous in the world.

The country's national league, *La Liga*, was founded in 1928–9 with ten clubs. It now has twenty. Apart from Real Madrid and Barcelona, some of the most famous clubs are: Atletico Madrid, Celta Vigo, Deportivo La Coruna, Real Betis, Sevilla, Valencia and Villareal. Barcelona won the first league competition. Real Madrid and Bilbao were other early winners.

The Spanish national team is known as *La Roja*, which means red, as the players wear a red (and yellow) strip[58]. After taking part in many European and World Cup competitions, Spain won the European Championship for the second time in 2008.

Great Spanish players of the past

Ricardo Zamora, a goalkeeper born in 1901, was one of the great players of the twentieth century. In his career, Zamora played for both Real Madrid and Barcelona. He helped these clubs to success and later managed several Spanish clubs.

Luis Suarez, born in 1935, played as a midfielder for several Spanish clubs and also for two Italian ones. He was named as the European Footballer of the Year in 1960. After he retired, Suarez had a second successful career as a manager.

Luis Aragones, born in Madrid in 1938, played as a striker. His career was spent in Spain and during his last ten years, he played 265 games for Atletico Madrid and scored 123 goals. He also played in the Spanish national team eleven times. Later, he was the manager of several Spanish clubs.

   He was also in charge of the successful Spanish national team that won the European Championship in 2008.

5

Football Goes West

Some of the greatest footballers in the world have come from the footballing countries of South America. The game has many fans there who take football very seriously.

A history of South American clubs and players

Argentina

Football is Argentina's most popular game. One of the most famous clubs is Boca Juniors, in the capital city of Buenos

Aires. The club's stadium is called *La Bombonera* – or 'The Chocolate Box' – because of its square shape. When the fans all jump up and down in the stadium, it shakes!

Two of the greatest players the world has ever seen came from Argentina.

The first is *Alfredo di Stéfano*. He played football for the River Plate club in the 1940s and, in 1953, he went to Spain to play for Real Madrid. He was there for ten years and helped the club to win the European Cup, now the Champions' League, five times.

The great English player, Sir Bobby Charlton, called Di Stephano 'the complete footballer'. 'The Blond Arrow', as Di Stephano was also called, influenced[59] every game he played in – in his home country and in Europe too. Di Stephano was very fit and did not retire until he was forty years old.

The second player is *Diego Maradona*. Most people have heard of Diego Maradona. Born in 1960, Maradona was powerful rather than graceful. He is only 1.68m, but he was a very quick player.

Maradona was born in a poor part of Buenos Aires and began playing football in the streets there. The boy was noticed by a football scout[60] at the age of ten and was playing professionally before he was sixteen.

In 1981, Maradona won his first medal, playing for Boca Juniors. Then, in June 1982, Maradona went to Europe to play for the Spanish club, FC Barcelona. His transfer fee was a record five million pounds.

In 1984, he went to the Italian club, Napoli, again for a record fee. Maradona helped Napoli to win many honours[61], but his greatest games were in international football.

Maradona played in the World Cup of 1982, but he is best remembered for the World Cup of 1986 when Argentina played England in a quarter-final and won 2–1. Maradona scored both goals, but the first was a handball – or the 'Hand

Diego Maradona playing for Argentina in the World Cup 1982, Spain

of God', as the Argentinian player called it. The referee did not see Maradona use his hand, but the English players did. They were very angry.

Then Maradona scored again to win the match. He ran half the length of the pitch, dribbling the ball past five English players. Then the little Argentinian shot the ball past the great English goalkeeper, Peter Shilton. Later, FIFA voted that second goal the greatest in the history of the World Cup.

This mixture of good and bad is typical of Maradona's career. He helped his country to win four World Cups and captained the national team sixteen times in that competition.

Maradona has also had problems with drugs and increased weight, but has been strong enough to fight them.

He has retired now, but took on the job as the Argentinian national coach and is still in the news.

When Maradona went to Calcutta, India, at the end of 2008, he was met by cheering crowds of fans. More than one hundred thousand of them filled the city's biggest stadium. Maradona laid the first stone of the city's soccer academy.

Brazil

Brazil is the home of beautiful football. Its players have always shown great skill on the pitch. Any team with a Brazilian player – in Brazil or Europe – is sure to play exciting football.

The first official match was played in Sao Paulo in 1894. Since then, Brazil has become a great footballing country. Its biggest stadium, one of the largest in the world, is the Maracana Stadium in Rio de Janeiro. The stadium can hold up to one hundred thousand fans.

Brazil has won the World Cup more times than any other country.

Pelé (*Edson Arantes do Nascimento*) is probably the greatest ever footballer. Pelé called football 'the beautiful game' and he was the game's most beautiful player.

Pelé was born in Tres Coracoes. His family was poor and Pelé made a little money by cleaning shoes. He was taught to play football by his father. A Brazilian player, de Brito, saw the eleven-year-old Pelé play football and said that he would one day be the greatest player in the world.

At the age of sixteen, Pelé scored a goal at his first appearance for Santos FC. At seventeen, he helped his country to win its first World Cup.

A few years later, many European clubs were trying to sign Pelé. But the Brazilian government declared him to be a 'national treasure[62]' to stop him leaving the country.

Pelé was not very tall, but he was fast and accurate. He was able to score goals with both feet and with his head too. In the 1970 World Cup Final against Italy, Pelé, aged twenty-nine, scored his hundredth goal.

Pelé played for the same club all his footballing career, from 1956 to 1974. Very few, if any, modern players can say that!

After his retirement, Pelé played in the North American Soccer League for two years. His plan was to make football – or soccer – popular in the USA. He succeeded and has been an ambassador for football ever since. A great player and a great man.

Mexico

Since 1927, the game in Mexico has been run[63] by the *Federación Mexicana de Fútbol*. Mexico took part in the 1928 Olympics and the country's team also played in the first World Cup competition in 1930. During the 1930s, the popularity of football in Mexico was increased by the arrival of Spanish people escaping from the Spanish Civil War.

Forty years later, in 1970, Mexico hosted[64] the World Cup and the home team got as far as the quarter-finals. The competition was held in Mexico again in 1986. For the second time, the home team reached the quarter-finals.

But Mexico could not take part in the 1990 World Cup because the country had been disqualified[65] from all international competitions for two years. It had been using players over the age of twenty-three in a youth competition, which was against FIFA rules.

Then Mexico reached the final of the *Copa America* in 1993, losing to Argentina 2–1.

The Swedish manager, Sven-Goran Eriksson was made manager of the Mexican national team in the summer of 2008. By February 2009, Eriksson was being blamed for Mexico's defeat by the USA in an early CONCACAF qualifying[66] group match for the 2010 World Cup. Eriksson said he needed more strikers. He felt sorry that too many Mexican footballers were playing in Europe, rather than staying in their own country.

Mexico then went on to beat Costa Rica. But when Honduras beat Mexico 3–1, leaving them in fourth place in their group, Eriksson was sacked[67].

It's not known whether Mexico gave the world the 'Mexican wave'. However, it became widely known after the 1986 World Cup, which was held in Mexico, when the wave was seen by millions of fans on television.

Hugo Sanchez played for Real Madrid for seven years, from 1985 to 1992, and was an important member of the great Spanish club. He was the manager of the Mexican national side before Sven-Goran Eriksson.

Uruguay

Uruguay is a small South American country with a big footballing reputation[68]. In 1930, the first World Cup was held

Football fans doing the Mexican wave

there and before the final between Uruguay and Argentina, there was an argument about the ball. Should it be provided by the host country or by Argentina? In the end, FIFA made the decision that Argentina's ball should be used in the first half and Uruguay's in the second half. The game, which took place in the Centario Stadium in Montevideo, was won 4–2 by the host team. Its captain was the great José Nasazzi.

Twenty years later, Uruguay beat Brazil 2–1 in the World Cup Final of 1950. The game was held in the Maracana Stadium in Brazil and the result was a great shock for the Brazilians.

Uruguay won gold medals in the Olympic Games of 1924 and 1928. The star of the 1924 Games was José Leandro Andrade, who was known as 'The Black Marvel[69]'. Andrade was very fast and a good defender too. The Olympics were held in Paris and Andrade was probably the first black player seen in Europe.

Uruguay's more recent successes have been in the *Copa America*.

43

USA

Football is called *soccer* in the United States because the game known as American football is more usual there. That game is much more like rugby.

But soccer has a longer history in the United States than most people think because immigrants from Europe preferred playing soccer to American football. By 1913, the United States had an association that was recognized by FIFA.

In 1921, the American Soccer League was founded. Some European clubs played in the United States and the USA took part in the first World Cup in 1930. The country played in later World Cup competitions too.

Foreign soccer teams continued to tour the USA. However, it was only in the second half of the twentieth century that soccer became popular throughout the country. In the World Cup of 1950, the USA beat England 1–0.

Television helped interest in the sport to grow in the United States. The World Cup was held in England in 1966 and many Americans watched the games on television.

The US national team played countries from Europe, South America and Russia too. Then, in 1994, the World Cup was held in the United States. The total number of people watching the games was more than three million.

Because of the size of the country, there were several different leagues. However, in the 1990s, they were brought together as the MLS – Major League Soccer.

In just a few years, soccer in the United States had become big business. Rich American men became owners of soccer clubs. These men have bought shares[70] in European clubs too.

By the first decade[71] of the twenty-first century, many men and women from England and Europe were playing soccer in the United States. The most famous is David Beckham, who was signed by LA Galaxy.

6

Football for All

Today, FIFA includes countries from all over the world, more than two hundred of them. The countries are in six big groups: Africa, Asia, North and Central America and the Caribbean, South America, Oceania and Europe.

Africa

Millions of people all over the world watch international matches on television. They can see club matches too. In many African countries, the games played in England's Premier League are very popular. Many young Africans are too poor to pay to watch their local club, so they watch football on television instead. And, of course, they play the game too, anywhere they can.

Many young African men and boys wear the shirt of their favourite club, usually one in the Premier League. Replica shirts can be seen everywhere in Africa and some English fans have sent out their own shirts to football-mad countries like Tanzania or Zambia.

Football is now a powerful force in Africa and it influences local politics and economics. The game brings pleasure to millions, but for the lucky few, it can bring money and fame too. The poorest boys dream of playing football in Europe. A few of them are lucky enough to do so and then they become heroes to millions.

When their football career is over, these players may become important politicians in their own countries. George Weah, for example, of Liberia, was named World Player of the Year in 1995. He then stood for election as his country's head of state. Though he was not successful, Weah has helped Liberia and the Liberian team in many ways.

Today many African footballers play in Europe. The Ghanaian midfielder, Michael Essien, plays for Chelsea along with Didier Drogba, his teammate from the Ivory Coast. The brothers Kolo and Yaya Toure, both Ivorians, play in England and Spain. Samuel Eto'o, from Cameroon, Jay-Jay Okocha and Obafemi Martins, both from Nigeria, are all established players.

Other important members of European teams include Ivorians Emmanuel Eboue and Johan Djourou (who has Swiss nationality), Alex Song from Cameroon and Emmanuel Adebayor, the African Player of the Year in 2008.

South Africa was banned by FIFA from 1964 until 1990 because of the country's policy of apartheid, which did not allow black and white footballers to play in the same teams. But South Africa, the host nation for the 2010 World Cup, has now rejected apartheid.

Politics and football cannot be separated in Africa or anywhere else in the world.

Asia

Asia, one of FIFA's six groups, is made up of nearly forty-five countries, as different in culture and distance as Afghanistan and Australia, Japan and Iraq, Bahrain and Thailand. But all of them are linked together by the power and popularity of football.

The big Premier League clubs are interested in finding future players from this group. They send scouts and go on pre-seasonal[72] tours to countries there.

Arsenal has close links with the Thai football club, Tero Sasana, and also offers coaching in England to young Indians whose ambition is to play football there. The president of

FIFA, Sepp Blatter, has called India the 'sleeping giant[73]' of football.

There has also been a suggestion that Premier League clubs should play an extra game in Asia every season.

The Middle East

The Middle East is showing interest in football too and some wealthy Middle Eastern businessmen are becoming involved in football management.

Manchester City Football Club is now owned by a rich Arab Group, based in Abu Dhabi.

Russia

In the old USSR, football teams were linked to various groups of workers and the teams were supported by the state. CSKA sports clubs had players from the Red Army. Dynamo was for the police, Spartak for trade unions and Locomotiv for the railway workers. These names were followed by the name of the city: Dynamo Moscow, Dynamo Kiev, Spartak Moscow, Locomotiv Moscow etc.

After the USSR was split into Russia and fourteen other states, football teams found private owners, but the clubs kept their old names. Many of these clubs compete in the big competitions. CSKA Moscow won the UEFA Cup in 2005 and Zenit St Petersburg, managed by the Dutchman, Dick Advocaat, won it in 2008.

Another Dutchman, Guus Hiddink, became the manager of the Russian national team in April 2006. He took the country to the semi-finals of the European Championship in 2008.

Russia and the other states – among them the Ukraine, Georgia and Belarus, all have their own national teams and they compete in the big international competitions.

Eastern Europe

Football is also very popular in Eastern Europe. Countries like Bulgaria and Croatia are hard to beat in international competitions. Some of their best players have been bought by Premier League clubs. These include Dimitar Berbatov, the Bulgarian striker, who was bought by Manchester United after a time with the London club, Tottenham Hotspur. Eduardo da Silva, also a striker, left his Croatian club, Dynamo Zagreb, to play for Arsenal. Eduardo was born in Brazil, but he has Croatian nationality.

Greece

Greece and Turkey are strong footballing nations too. Greece's best-known teams are Panathinaikos and Olympiakos.

Greece was the unexpected winner of the European Championship 2004, when they beat the host side, Portugal, in the final.

The Greek national team celebrating at the final of the European Championship 2004, Portugal

Turkey

Boys first began playing football in Galatasaray High School, Istanbul, in 1905 and the Galatasaray club was founded in 1923. This was the same year that the Turkish Football Federation (TFF) was formed. The TFF joined FIFA in 1923 and UEFA in 1962. The federation is in charge of the national team and the Turkish football leagues.

Professional football started in Turkey in 1951. The country now has more than five thousand clubs – both amateur and professional – and women play the game too.

Turkey now has many fans who take their football very seriously. All the country's big cities have stadiums. The biggest belongs to Galatasaray, in Istanbul. This stadium holds more than eighty thousand fans. Many important matches, including Champions' League Finals, have been played there. Visiting teams who play in the stadiums of Istanbul find it a very noisy experience. The fans of the Istanbul teams, Fenerbahce and Galatasaray, must be some of the noisiest in the world!

The Turkish national team played their first match against Romania in 1923. Mustapha Kemal Ataturk, the founder and first president of the Turkish Republic, was a great fan of the game and he was there to see them play. The Turkish national team has had good times and bad. It has qualified for the World Cup several times. Its best result[74] was reaching third place in 2002. The team has also taken part in several European Championship and Confederations Cup competitions.

Most of the players in the national side play for Turkish clubs – usually the big Istanbul ones – Galatasaray and Fenerbahce.

Other top Turkish footballers play for foreign clubs in Europe and Russia. There are also players from all over the world who are important members of Turkish clubs. Turkey is part of the international world of football.

7

Women's Football

Today, football is a popular sport with women. Many go to matches and know a lot about the game. They play the game too and there are women's leagues in Britain and all over the world. Every year, the women's game becomes more and more popular.

The very first match between two women's teams took place in England in 1895. The year before, Miss Nettie Honeyball had founded the British Ladies' Football Club. About thirty women wanted to play for the club. They practised hard because Miss Honeyball wanted to show men that women were not just 'ornamental[75] and useless'. They played games in many parts of Britain. Sometimes the spectators laughed at them, but Miss Honeyball and her friends did not care. More women's clubs were founded during and after the First World War.

The first international match took place in 1920. An English team based in Preston, in the north of England, played a French side in a charity[76] match. Later that year, at Christmas, two northern teams played before a crowd of fifty-three thousand people. Things were looking good for women's football.

Then, a year later, the FA banned women from playing on Football League grounds. The FA said, 'The game of football is quite unsuitable for females and ought not[77] to be encouraged.'

Some women went on playing, but very few people supported them. The FA ban was not lifted for another fifty years!

But in 1969, the Women's Football Association was formed. It was made up of forty-four clubs. It slowly gained support, but was not fully accepted by the FA until the 1990s.

In 1998, the FA held a UEFA conference on Women and Football and in 2002, it announced that football was the most important sport for women in the country.

By that time, women's football was very popular in the USA too. Mia Hamm, born in 1972, twice won FIFA's Women's World Player of the Year Award, in 2001 and 2002. She helped her country to win the FIFA Women's World Cup in 1991.

In England, famous women players include Faye White, Rachel Yankey and Julia Fleeting. Kelly Smith and Alex Scott have moved on to a US club, the Boston Breakers.

Women's leagues have now been set up all over the world and the game is popular in Europe, parts of Africa and Asia. Women's football is now played internationally with both grace and skill.

Japan playing Argentina in the Women's World Cup 2007, China

8

Football in the Modern Day

In 1985, Liverpool reached the final of what was then called the European Cup, which they had won the year before. They were playing the Italian club, Juventus.

The match took place in the old Heysel Stadium in Brussels. One hour before the match started, there was trouble between the Liverpool fans and the Italians. An old wall collapsed and thirty-nine people were killed. Hundreds were injured. The Liverpool fans were blamed and English clubs were banned from all European competitions. The ban was lifted in the 1990–1 season, with Liverpool allowed back a year later.

15th April 1989 was another sad day for English football and for Liverpool. By that time, thousands of people in England went to big matches every week. Thousands more watched football on television.

At that time, fans all stood on the terraces and sometimes these fans tried to make matches more exciting by running onto the pitch or even fighting rival fans. To stop this happening, wire fences had been put up between the terraces and the pitch in English stadiums.

A match was to be played at the Hillsborough Stadium, the home of Sheffield Wednesday. Liverpool was playing Nottingham Forest in the semi-final of the FA Cup.

The semi-final was due to begin at 3pm, the usual time for a Saturday match. Many fans arrived late because of unexpected roadworks, and they all arrived at the same time. The fans all wanted to get into the stadium quickly before the match started.

The queues were getting longer and so the police opened a big gate. The fans hurried through the tunnel in front of them.

But the nearby terraces were full.

The whistle blew for kick-off and the fans began to push forward. The wire fences held them back for a time and then the fences broke. People fell onto the pitch and on top of each other. They could not breathe and some were crushed to death.

Many people watched this on television, but at first, no one understood what was happening. The match was stopped, but it was too late. Ninety-six people died and hundreds more were injured.

Over twenty years have gone by, but what happened at Hillsborough has not been forgotten. On the afternoon of 15th April 2009, thousands of Liverpool fans went to Anfield, their home stadium. They wanted to remember the ninety-six people who lost their lives.

Because of this sad event, fans are no longer allowed to stand in the terraces. Everyone has a numbered seat and has to sit on it. Stadiums hold fewer people, but they are much safer.

Player power

Modern players are probably fitter than many of those who played football in the past. Then many players smoked – even at half time! Players were also much heavier than the slim, fit footballers of today.

There is a reason for this. As well as training hard, modern players must think about their diet[78] and way of life. Football, especially in the Premier League, is played at a very fast pace[79] and some players may run ten or more kilometres during one match.

Modern players are different in another way too. For example, a player used to play only for clubs in his own country. He might stay with the same club for his whole career. Clubs could sign only a limited number of foreign players.

These days, a good player is able to join clubs in other countries. This is important for players who live in the EU[80].

In 1995, a Belgian footballer called Jean-Marc Bosman wanted to move from his Belgian club, Liege, to play for a French club, Dunkerque. His contract with Liege had ended, so Dunkerque refused to pay a transfer fee for Bosman. Liege decided that he couldn't leave unless Dunkerque paid them money. Bosman said that he was free to move within the EU and that players without a contract should be allowed to move freely too.

Bosman took his case[81] to the European Court and won. Transfer fees for out-of-contract players were now illegal between EU countries. Fees would only be paid when the players' contract had not ended. The court also decided that clubs could buy as many EU players as they liked.

The players (and their agents[82]) now had more power than the clubs. They could ask for a longer contract. They could ask for higher wages too, and the clubs had to pay them if they wanted to keep the player.

This meant that fans had to pay more money for their tickets, but they got the chance to see more European players play for their club.

Today, more and more foreign players are joining Premier League clubs from non-European countries too. Some of the clubs do not have any English players on the pitch at all. In Europe, clubs are also buying more and more foreign players. It is a problem for all European countries, not just Britain.

The president of FIFA, Sepp Blatter, is very unhappy about this and Michel Platini, the president of UEFA, agrees with him.

Blatter wants to bring in what he calls the 'six plus five rule'. This would mean that every team playing in a match would have six or more 'home' players in it and not more than five foreign ones. Would this be legal or not? No one seems to know.

———

Some European players stay with Premier League clubs for a long time and become popular with the fans. The fans enjoy watching their favourite players' skilful game, week after week, and the players enjoy playing their football in England.

Thierry Henry joined Arsenal in 1999 and stayed with the club for eight years, during which time he became their top scorer with 226 goals, beating Ian Wright's record of 184 goals.

Henry delighted the North London club with hours of brilliant football when he was a striker there. He was also the club's captain for two years. He then moved to Barcelona.

Cesc Fabregas, the young Spanish player, was only sixteen when he joined Arsenal from Barcelona in 2003. This strong, clever midfielder soon became an important member of the team. He was made club captain in 2008.

In the same year, Fabregas was part of the Spanish national team that won the European Championship.

Cristiano Ronaldo joined Manchester United in 2003, aged eighteen. The Portuguese striker soon showed that he could play very well with the English striker, Wayne Rooney, and his other teammates.

Ronaldo has already won many awards, helped his club to win Premier League titles and played in his own country's national team. In 2009, he signed for Real Madrid. The Spanish club paid a record eighty million pounds for him.

Are these players and others like them keeping English players from playing for English teams? Not always. The big clubs all have academies where young English footballers can be trained and educated too. Many of them go on to be great players. But, of course, they may leave to play for foreign clubs!

The power of the big clubs

The English Premier League is thought to be one of the best, so young players from all over the world want to play in it.

The big clubs have scouts who travel to lots of different countries around the world looking for young talent. These men often find great young players in the many countries of Africa, South America and, more recently, Asia.

Many of these young players quickly become very rich and famous, and millions of fans are able to admire their skills. But when they leave their country, their local clubs lose a good player and the growth of the game can suffer there.

Cups and competitions

Today's fans want their teams to be international – they want the best. They want their teams to win matches. They want them to win cups.

First of all, clubs want to win cups in their own countries. Every club wants to be top of their own league and win that important cup, or at least be in the top four of their league.

Domestic cups are fought for in every league and in every country. One of the most famous of them all is England's FA Cup. The FA Cup has been competed for in England since the 1871–2 season, when fifteen clubs took part.

In the 2008–9 season, seven hundred clubs entered! Although the cup is usually won by a Premier League club, there can be surprises, as clubs from all the domestic leagues take part. Forty-two different clubs have won the trophy[83] so far.

The final of the FA Cup is played at the national stadium, Wembley, in north-west London. The first Wembley Stadium was ready for the 1923 game between Bolton Wanderers and West Ham United. Two hundred thousand people crowded into the stadium, but there was no trouble (Bolton won 2–0).

A new Wembley Stadium has now been built and the FA Cup Final was held there for the first time in 2007. It was between two great teams – Manchester United and Chelsea. Chelsea won in extra time, with the Ivorian player, Didier Drogba, scoring the only goal. There were 89,826 fans in the stadium.

The Champions' League

The UEFA Champions' League was first held under that name in the 1992–3 season. Before that, the competition was called the European Champion Clubs' Cup or just the European Cup.

The way that the competition is organized[84] has changed several times. Today, after the qualifying matches, there is a group stage[85] – eight groups of four clubs that play each other twice.

The first and second clubs from each group go on to the knockout[86] stage. Each club is drawn[87] against one other club which it plays twice, 'over two legs' – home and away. The matches are won on aggregate[88] and away goals count for double if there is a draw. Games may go to extra time and penalties.

The eight winners go on to the quarter and semi-finals. Two teams then go on to play each other in the final.

The clubs in the competition have to play a lot of games. But the Champions' League is an important competition to win. Success brings the winning club a lot of money and the best players want to play there.

Michel Platini, president of UEFA, requested changes in the competition, which were made in the 2009–10 season. These changes mean that more clubs can take part. He thinks that the big clubs in every country may have become too important.

How are these clubs chosen in the first place? They must have won their own domestic league or have been placed near the top – usually in the first four. That is why the league title is so important in every European country.

In recent years, Real Madrid has been the most successful club in the Champions' League, but Liverpool, Manchester United, AC Milan and FC Barcelona have also won the title in the past few years.

Clubs who do not get beyond the group stage of the Champions' League are among those that compete for the UEFA Cup, which became the UEFA Europa League in the 2009–10 season. This competition is organized in much the same way as the Champions' League.

 The *Copa Libertadores* is the 'Champions' League' of South America. Argentinian teams have won it twenty-one times in the forty-nine years it has been fought for. A team from Ecuador won the cup in 2008 for the first time, but Brazilian teams are doing well now.

Even though many Brazilian players leave to go abroad, Brazil has a bigger population than all the other South American countries added together. Local and international football games are now shown on television, of course, and this means more money for the clubs.

The international cups

Countries play for cups too. The national teams all want to win the World Cup. Then there are regional competitions for cups – the European Championship, the African Cup, the *Copa Americana* etc.

The European Championship, which is for countries not clubs, is held by UEFA every four years. The competition is also known as UEFA Euro followed by the year – 2004 … 2008 … 2012.

This championship is never held in the same year as the World Cup, which is numbered by the year in the same way – 2006 … 2010 … 2014 …

Countries bid[89] for a chance to hold the competitions and the successful country (or sometimes countries) must have enough suitable stadiums. The qualifying matches take months to complete. They lead on to the group and knockout stages.

Orlando Stadium, Soweto, built for the 2010 World Cup, South Africa

The first modern Olympic Games were held in 1896. These games were only for amateurs under the age of twenty-three. At that time, football in England was played by both amateurs and professionals, and that was a problem which was not sorted out for some time.

In 1930, the first World Cup was played for and that soon became more important for both amateur and professional footballers. However, by the 1980s, professionals could play in the Olympic Games too.

9

Money, Money, Money

In the twenty-first century, football has become big business. The game is ruled by money. But where does the money come from and where does it go? Without the fans, football would have no future. Every season, fans of Premier League clubs have to pay a great deal of money for their tickets. They pay for the replica shirts, scarves and badges[90] that they buy from the club shop.

The Premier League was founded in 1992. By January 2009, the gates of the clubs had let in more than two hundred million fans. What do the fans get for their money? They get a lot – the best English players and managers, and great players and managers from all over the world too.

The importance of the manager

Footballers from different countries play in different ways. A mixture of styles allows managers to use their players in many different formations. Clever managers can use their team's strengths to show up the weaknesses of rival teams. A good manager can use his substitutes in a skilful way too. The manager has seven players 'on the bench' and he can use up to three of these substitutes as tactical[91] replacements. A striker could replace a defender if more goals were needed. On the other hand, another strong defender might help to win the match.

Football is a team game. However great the individual players, they must all work together as a team and for the team. It is the manager's job to see that this happens. Managers have to be very strong people. They are always blamed if things go wrong. They are often sacked too, because in the modern game success and money go together.

Since the 1970s, many managers have become as famous as the players. These managers may have been great footballers, like Kevin Keegan or Alan Shearer. Or they may have had a short career as players but gone on to become great managers.

Great managers of the past

Brian Clough was the outspoken[92] Englishman who began his management career at Derby. Then he went to Leeds, but was sacked after only forty-four days when the players turned against[93] him. Moving on to Nottingham Forest in 1975, Clough led the team to promotion[94], two European Cups, an English league cup and an English league championship. People either loved Clough or hated him. A film has been made about his career. He was, perhaps, the first celebrity[95] manager.

Rinus Michels was the great Dutch manager who was named by FIFA as Coach of the Century in 1999. Michels, who was known as 'The General', once said that 'football is war'.

Before becoming a manager, Michels had a successful career as a player for his club, Ajax, and for his country too.

He then became a manager and, led by Michels, Ajax won the European Cup in 1971. Later, he helped Barcelona to win the Spanish league title.

As manager of the Dutch national team, Michels never won the World Cup, but the team reached the final in 1974 and 1978. In 1988, his team won the European Championship.

Michels was lucky to have many great Dutch footballers playing for him and, in the early 1970s, he developed the idea of 'total football'. He allowed skilful players like Johan Cruyff to play freely, all over the pitch, and change the pace of the game as they wished.

Carlos Bianchi played as a striker in both Argentina and France, where he was the leading goalscorer for five seasons. His career as a manager began in France in 1984 and he managed clubs in that country until 1993.

Returning to Argentina, Bianchi won several cups with the club Velez, and, after a time in Italy, he became a very successful manager of Boca Juniors. He helped the club to win the *Copa Libertadores* three times in four years.

Bianchi was named as South American Manager of the Year five times – in 1994, 1998, 2000, 2001 and 2003. He ended his career with a short time at Atletico Madrid before retiring in 2006.

Carlos Alberto Parreira is a Brazilian manager who never played professional football. Before becoming a manager, he was a fitness coach.

Although he is most closely linked to the Brazilian club, Fluminense, Parreira managed the national team too – in 1994, when Brazil won the World Cup, and again in 2006. In total, Parreira has managed no fewer than five national teams in their bids to win the World Cup. However, Parreira could not take Brazil any further than the quarter-finals of the World Cup in 2006 and he resigned in July of that year.

He was given the job as the South African manager for the 2010 World Cup, but owing to his wife's illness, he resigned in 2008 and returned to Brazil. There he became manager of Fluminense, with whom he had won domestic cups in 1984 and 1999.

———

Football managers have always had many problems. They have to please their club, the players and of course, the fans.

Today their greatest problem may be the club's owner. The owner is a very rich man – he has to be. He has bought the club as a business and he wants it to make money. That means winning matches and winning international titles too.

The Premier League has recently begun to question 'football's relationship with money'. This means that owners should be asked about their interest in football before they can take control of a club. Are they doing it because they love the game or just to make money?

All owners want to have the very best players and they are prepared to pay a lot of money for them. The manager may not think they are the right players for his team, but the owner is used to getting what he wants.

So there may be arguments and the manager may get the sack or decide to leave for another club. Some of the players that the manager has chosen may leave with him.

Because of all these problems, modern managers often change the club they work for. Big clubs are prepared to pay big money to get the best managers, whatever their nationality.

There is a small group of first-class football managers in the world and some of them change their job every two or three years, just as many players do. A few stay loyal to one club.

All these men are alike in one thing. They have to be very tough!

Great modern managers

Sir Alex Ferguson is different from most modern managers. He has been in charge of just one club, Manchester United, since 1986.

Sir Alex, who is Scottish, was born in Glasgow in 1941. He began playing football as a striker in 1957 and played for several Scottish teams, including the Glasgow club, Rangers. In 1974, he became a manager for the first time and from 1978 to 1986, he was in charge at the Scottish club, Aberdeen. After a year as temporary[96] manager of the national team, Ferguson became manager of Manchester United.

His first three years at the club were disappointing and fans asked for him to be sacked. But Ferguson stayed and went on to become the most successful manager of any English club.

Sir Alex has brought stability[97] to a club which has many fine players, but he has always said that no player is bigger than the club. Manchester United has won all the domestic cups many times and has been very successful in the Champions' League too.

Like Brian Clough, Sir Alex is very outspoken. His great experience has given him power and influence and people listen to what he says.

Manchester United is one of the richest clubs in the world and is able to buy the very best players. The club has fans everywhere!

Sir Alex Ferguson managing Manchester United

The Frenchman, *Arsene Wenger,* has been manager of Arsenal since 1996. After a short football career, Wenger worked as a manager in France (AS Nancy), Monaco and Japan (Nagoya Grampus Eight).

In spite of his success with the English club, Wenger has sometimes been criticized for using too many foreign players. His reply is that he looks at a player's ability[98], not his passport.

He is well-known for buying young, unknown players and turning them into stars.

José Mourinho, the Portuguese manager who calls himself 'The Special One' is the son of a footballer. Young José became a footballer too, but he soon decided that he would have more success as a manager.

When the great Englishman, Bobby Robson, became manager of the Portuguese club, Sporting Lisbon, he asked Mourinho to become his translator and assistant coach. They became friends and when Robson moved to Porto, Mourinho went with him. Later the two men worked together at Barcelona.

Mourinho returned to Porto in 2002 and in 2004, the club won the Champions' League. The following year, he went to the West London club, Chelsea. He has twice been named as the Worlds's Best Football Manager.

Mourinho made friends at Chelsea, but enemies too. He left after three years to go to the Italian club, Inter Milan. He says that he enjoys the risk[99] of being a manager because he never knows when he may be sacked!

Carlo Ancelotti became the manager of Inter Milan's greatest rival, AC Milan, in 2001. He had previously managed other Italian clubs, including Juventus. Before he became a manager, Ancelotti had a very successful career as a player with three Italian teams – Parma, Roma and AC Milan. At the Milan club, he was part of the great team that won the European Cup in 1989 and 1990.

Ancelotti has been equally successful as manager of AC Milan, winning the Champions' League twice. In the summer of 2009, he agreed to become manager of Chelsea.

Guus Hiddink has shown in his career that the nationality of a football manager is not important, whether he is managing a club or a national team.

After playing for several clubs in the Netherlands and the USA, Hiddink managed two Dutch clubs. He helped PSV Eindhoven become one of the best Dutch clubs and they won the European Cup in 1988.

After some time in Turkey and Spain, Hiddink returned to his home country, the Netherlands, where he was asked to manage the national team. They reached the semi-finals of the 1998 World Cup, but Hiddink resigned.

Hiddink then returned to Spain, but was not very successful there. His next international job was in South Korea, which was one of the host nations for the 2002 World Cup. He was popular in South Korea and did well there.

Hiddink then took charge of the Australian national team until 2006. Next, he became the Russian manager and, for a short time, he managed Chelsea too.

As we have seen, national teams now look all over the world for their managers. For example, Sven-Goran Eriksson was made the first foreign manager of the English national team in 2001.

The president of FIFA, Sepp Blatter, was shocked that the FA had chosen the Swede rather than an Englishman to lead the national team. However, Eriksson had successfully managed clubs in Europe and he stayed with the English team until 2006, taking charge of sixty-seven games.

England went out of the 2006 World Cup at the quarter-final stage and Eriksson left too. He returned after a year to manage Manchester City, but was sacked after two years by the club's rich owner.

Eriksson then took over as manager of Mexico's national team, but was sacked after some bad results.

Fabio Capello was the next foreign manager of the English team after it failed to qualify for the European Championship 2008 under an English manager.

The Italian came to England in 2007 after a very successful career. He had already been the manager of four of Europe's best clubs – AC Milan, Roma and Juventus in Italy and Real Madrid in Spain.

Capello won the domestic league title with all these clubs and he helped AC Milan to win the Champions' League in 1994 in an exciting final against Barcelona.

Capello expects discipline[100] and hard work from his players. He gets it too.

Manager or coach?

In modern football, the manager decides on the kind of team he wants and plans how it can improve.

The best managers work as coaches too. With their assistants helping them, they join their players on the training pitch. So the manager makes plans and, as the coach, makes sure that they are carried out.

———

The strongest teams have players from all over the world and the clubs spend a lot of money training them. That is why television has become so important.

Clubs like their matches to be shown on television because the television companies pay the clubs well. And fans can watch their teams play.

This is especially true of the English Premier League. Its matches are watched on television by fans all over the world. All the fans see the sponsors' names and logos on the players' shirts. The sponsors are pleased and so are the clubs, because the sponsors pay them well.

But television can be a problem too – especially for referees. They have to decide in seconds when to give a penalty or whether the ball has gone over the goal-line. Sometimes the referee makes a mistake. The incident[101] is replayed on television and may be seen all over the world, but it is too late. His decision may have changed the result of the match.

Technology is used in other sports. Why not in football? FIFA says that its use will weaken the power of the referee. But wrong decisions upset the players and the fans. The clubs may also lose a lot of money if the wrong decision is made.

The clubs need all the money that they can get. They spend a lot of it on training, but there are other things too. They may want to build a new, bigger stadium that will hold more fans, or they may want to improve an old one.

A great deal of the clubs' money is spent on buying players from other clubs. Big players mean big transfer fees. Then, if the transfer is successful, the players' wages will be very high.

In 2009, an attempt was made by Manchester City to buy the Brazilian player, Kaká, for a reported one hundred million pounds from AC Milan. Kaká stayed in Milan, but he later agreed to go to Real Madrid for sixty-two million pounds.

Michel Platini, the president of UEFA, thinks that offers like this are wrong. He also thinks that all players' wages should be capped – there should be a limit on the amount of money that the best players can earn.

But who are the 'best' players? And how long can they stay at the top? David Beckham, born in 1975, has won a record number of caps for England. The great French player, Zinedine Zidane, went on playing internationally until he was thirty-four.

But most first-class footballers have much shorter careers than Beckham or Zidane. These days, the game is so fast that only the fittest players can go on playing after the age of thirty-five. The fans should enjoy their favourite players' skills while they can.

Top clubs have to spend a lot of money on finding and training young players to replace their stars when they retire. All big clubs have football academies in which boys and girls are trained from the age of nine. As they get older, these young footballers play in the Under-18 and Under-21 leagues against other clubs.

These youth leagues help young footballers to compete and develop their skills. Their aim is to be good enough to play in their club's first team.

The football academies give young people a good education too. The biggest clubs have academies in other countries as well as their own.

———

Here are a few facts about some young players who may be the stars of tomorrow. Some of them are already playing first-class football.

Anderson (Luis de Abreu Oliveira) was born in Brazil in 1988. Praised by Sir Alex Ferguson, this skilful central midfielder settled well into European football. He has also played for his country.

Macauley Chrisantus was born in Nigeria in 1991. Chrisantus is a powerful striker who began his career with the German club, SV Hamburg.

Bojan Krkic was born in Spain in 1990. This young striker plays first-class football and has already won caps for his country. He has been compared to the Dutchman, Johan Cruyff.

Toni Kroos was born in Germany in 1990. He is an attacking

69

midfielder who won the Golden Ball in FIFA's Under-17 World Cup in 2007.

Federico Macheda was born in Italy in 1991. The young striker has already played in Manchester United's first team and scored match-winning goals.

Lionel Messi was born in Argentina in 1987. Messi is a star player in Spain's *La Liga* and he has also played for his national team. He has been compared to Maradona, who has praised Messi's football.

David N'Gog was born in France in 1989. N'Gog scored several goals in French youth teams. He was soon signed by Liverpool.

Alexandre Pato was born in Brazil in 1989. David Beckham believes that this talented striker will be one of the great players of the future.

Aaron Ramsey was born in Wales in 1990. Ramsey has played for his country in their Under-21 team and for Arsenal, his first Premier League club.

Giovanni Dos Santos was born in Mexico in 1989. He was signed early in his career by the London club, Tottenham Hotspur.

Carlos Vela was also born in Mexico in 1989. Vela is a lively young striker who scored five goals to help Mexico win the Under-17 FIFA World Cup in 2005. Vela himself won the Golden Boot and later, a place in Arsenal's first team.

Theo Walcott was born in England in 1989 and picked out by Arsene Wenger to play for Arsenal. The fast-moving striker is an important Premier League player and he has played for England too.

Jack Wilshere was born in England in 1992. Jack joined Arsenal aged nine. He is a clever midfielder who has already played for the first team.

———

People often complain that top footballers get too much money. They live in very large houses and have very rich lifestyles. They buy expensive cars and wear designer clothes.

But many footballers also give time and money to help the local communities. In multicultural areas of big cities, foreign players go into schools and help young pupils with their French, Spanish or Italian lessons. Players visit children in hospitals and youth clubs too.

Players often use their money to help people in their own countries. The family of Patrick Viera, the great French player, comes from Senegal, West Africa. Together with two other footballing friends, Viera set up the Diambars Academy in Saly, near the capital city Dakar, in 2003. There, African boys learn to read and write and then to play football. Similar academies have been set up by players in other African countries.

Football academies have also been started by other famous players like David Beckham and Cesc Fabregas in their home countries. In these ways, many footballers help young people to enjoy playing football and have better lives.

Football for all – all for football

All over the world young people play football because they enjoy the game. They may not be very good and they may not become famous, but they want to play. They may play in muddy fields or on a dusty street. Their parents or other adults help them. They learn from playing and perhaps from watching games at their local club or on television. They learn to love football and football could not go on without them. They are the players and fans of the future.

Enjoy the game!

David Beckham training young players at the David Beckham Football Academy, London

Points for Understanding

1

1 How long have young people been playing ball games?
2 Where were the earliest ball games played?
3 How many teams were there in early ball games?
4 How many players were there in each team and who were the players?
5 How did these games end?
6 What did the fans do at the end of these games?
7 Where were these games played: (a) kemari (b) harpastum?

2

1 Complete these sentences:
   (a) The kings of England did not like football. It was not
   ....
   (b) A headmaster liked the game because it taught boys
   to .... and ....
   (c) In rugger, players could take .... and
   ....
2 When and where was the Football Association founded?
3 How many rules did it make and when were they first used?
4 Complete these sentences:
   (a) The goal did not have .... or
   ....
   (b) Referees did not have .... or
   ....
   (c) The ball and the players' boots were very ....

3

1 Say what happened:
   (a) In 1888 ....
   (b) By 1894 ....
   (c) In 1898 ....
2 Can the official rules of football ever be changed? Explain your
   answer.
3 When and where was the first stadium in England built?
4 Why was 22nd January 1927 an important day for football?
5 Which player always wears the number one shirt and how is this
   player's shirt different?
6 When did the FA first let players wear numbers on their shirts?
7 When were substitutes for injured players first allowed?
8 Which great British players were never given red or yellow cards?

4

1 In the game of football, what is the difference between an amateur
   and a professional player?
2 How did football spread to Europe and South America?
3 Why did FAs start different leagues?
4 What is FIFA and when was it founded?
5 How many countries now belong to FIFA?
6 Name the European players known as: (a) Zizou   (b) The Cat
   (c) The Blond Bomber and give the positions they played in.
7 In which cities are these clubs based: (a) Lazio   (b) Juventus?
8 Name the English teams that Zola: (a) played for   (b) managed.
9 The players of one European national team wear orange shirts.
   Which country do they play for?
10 Several Dutch footballers played for an Italian club at the same
   time. Name the club and the players.
11 Which great Portuguese player was not born in Portugal?
12 What is the Spanish national league called and when was it
   founded?

5

1. Name the famous Argentinian footballer who played for Real Madrid.
2. Name the Argentinian who played for Boca Juniors. Where is this team based?
3. This player played in Europe too. Which teams did he play for?
4. Why did Pelé never play for a European club?
5. Why were 1970 and 1993 important years for Mexican football?
6. Name the Uruguayan player known as The Black Marvel.
7. Why is football usually called soccer in the United States?
8. A famous English footballer has played for an American club. Name: (a) the player   (b) the club.

6

1. How many groups are FIFA's countries divided into?
2. In which group is football most closely linked to politics?
3. Many African footballers play in Europe. Give the names of three of them and the countries they come from.
4. Premier League clubs are interested in Asian footballers. How do we know this?
5. Which two Russian clubs have done well in the UEFA Cup?
6. Two strikers from Eastern Europe have played for English clubs. Name: (a) the players   (b) the clubs.
7. Give the names of: (a) two famous Greek clubs (b) two famous Turkish ones.

7

1. What did Miss Nettie Honeyball do in 1894?
2. Why did she want women to play football?
3. Why did the FA not want women to play the game?
4. By 2002 the FA had changed its mind about women's football. What did the FA say about it?
5. Mia Hamm was an important player for which country?
6. Which award did she win twice?

8

1 What happened in 1985 that meant English clubs were banned for several years from European competitions?
2 Why is 15th April 1989 remembered as a sad day for English football?
3 What changes were made to stadiums afterwards?
4 How do modern players differ from those of the past?
5 Why was Jean-Marc Bosman an important player?
6 How would the six plus five rule change football?
7 How do English clubs help English boys and girls to become good footballers?
8 How do these clubs find good young foreign players?
9 What is the difference between a domestic cup and an international cup? Give an example of each.
10 Why is the Champions' League so important?
11 How often are the World Cup and the European Championship competed for?
12 What must countries have to host an international cup?

9

1 Why are fans so important to football?
2 Who may cause problems for managers in modern football? What do managers often do as a result?
3 Choose three modern managers and write down three facts about each of them.
4 Why is television so important to modern football?
5 Why do referees sometimes find television a problem?
6 What does Michel Platini think about high wages for players?
7 What does he want to do about it?
8 What are the top footballers' lifestyles like?
9 How do rich players help boys and girls who want to be great footballers too?

Glossary

1 **ancient** (page 6)
   relating to a period of history a very long time ago
2 **slave** (page 6)
   someone who belongs by law to another person and who has to work for this person
3 **figure** (page 6)
   a small copy of a person or animal
4 **pad** (page 6)
   a thick piece of soft material that you use for protecting something, making it more comfortable or changing its shape
5 **sacrifice** (page 7)
   the act of killing a person or animal in the name of a special god
6 **priest** (page 7)
   a man who performs religious duties in some religions that are not Christian
7 **banned** – *to ban something* (page 7)
   to say officially that something is illegal or not allowed
8 **flick** (page 7)
   a sudden quick movement
9 **inflated** – *to inflate something* (page 7)
   to fill something with air or gas
10 **bladder** (page 7)
   the part inside the body where urine – liquid waste from a person's or animal's body – collects
11 **kit** (page 7)
   special clothes that you wear for a sport
12 **record** (page 8)
   information that is kept about something that has happened
13 **archery** (page 9)
   the sport of shooting *arrows* from a *bow*. An *arrow* is a weapon in the form of a thin straight stick with a sharp point at one end and feathers at the other. It is fired using a round piece of wood called a *bow*.
14 **defended** – *to defend something* (page 9)
   to try to stop members of the other team from scoring

15 *association* (page 10)
an organization for people who have similar interests or aims
16 *trip up* – *to trip someone up* (page 11)
to make someone hit their foot on something and fall down
17 *opponent* (page 11)
someone who is competing against you
18 *sponsor* (page 12)
a person or business that pays for something such as an event, a team or a radio or television programme as a way of advertising their company or products
19 *revised* – *to revise something* (page 14)
to change or add to something, or make it better
20 *rival* (page 15)
a person, team or business that competes with another
21 *chant* (page 15)
to shout or sing a word or phrase many times
22 *commentary* (page 16)
a spoken description of an event that is given as the event is happening, especially on the radio or television. A person whose job is to give such a description is called a *commentator*.
23 *synthetic* (page 17)
made from artificial material
24 *material* (page 17)
used for making things such as clothes
25 *swerve* (page 17)
to change direction suddenly
26 *manufacturer* (page 17)
a person or company that makes a certain type of product, especially in a factory
27 *formation* (page 17)
a pattern that people or things are arranged into
28 *rejected* – *to reject something* (page 18)
to not accept or agree with something such as an idea or an argument
29 *replica* (page 19)
a very careful copy of something
30 *retired* – *to retire* (page 19)
to stop working permanently, especially when you are old
31 *wizard* (page 19)
someone who is very good at something

32 *accurate* (page 19)
   correct in every detail, and without any mistakes
33 *assist* (page 19)
   something done by a player that helps another player in the same
   team to score a point or goal
34 *knighted* – *to be knighted* (page 20)
   to be given a *knighthood* – an honour given by a British king or
   queen that allows a man to use the title 'Sir' before his name
35 *skilful* (page 20)
   showing a lot of *skill* – the ability to do something well, usually as a
   result of experience and training
36 *suffered* – *to suffer from something* (page 20)
   to have an illness or a problem
37 *babe* (page 22)
   an informal word for a baby. *The Busby Babes* were like Matt Busby's
   babies because he trained them.
38 *talented* (page 22)
   very good at something
39 *anticipation* (page 22)
   the skill of guessing what will happen next and being ready to act
40 **OBE** (page 23)
   Officer of the Order of the British Empire: a special title given to
   someone in the UK whose work has helped the country
41 *lifestyle* (page 23)
   the type of life that someone has, for example the type of things
   that they own and the type of activities that they do
42 *loyal* (page 23)
   someone who is *loyal* continues to support a person, organization or
   idea in difficult times
43 *domestic* (page 24)
   relating to the country being talked about
44 *industrial* (page 24)
   an *industrial* region or country has a lot of *industries* in it – all the
   businesses that make a certain thing
45 *invented* – *to invent something* (page 24)
   to design or create something that did not exist before
46 *engineer* (page 24)
   someone who designs things such as roads, railways or machines
47 *standard* (page 25)
   a level of quality or success that is used for judging someone or
   something

48 **replaced** – *to replace someone or something* (page 25)
to get rid of someone or something and put a new person or thing in their place
49 **multicultural** (page 27)
including people of different cultures
50 **insulted** – *to insult someone* (page 28)
to say or do something that is rude
51 **graceful** (page 29)
smooth and beautiful
52 **immigrant** (page 30)
someone who comes to live in a country from another country
53 **in spite of** (page 30)
used when talking about a fact that makes something else surprising
54 **lap of honour** (page 34)
a slow run around a sports field that the winner makes after a race or game
55 **colony** (page 35)
a country that is controlled by another country
56 **praised** – *to praise someone or something* (page 35)
to express strong positive opinions or respect for someone or something
57 **transfer** (page 36)
the process of moving, or being moved, from one job or place to another
58 **strip** (page 36)
a uniform that the players in a team wear
59 **influenced** – *to influence someone or something* (page 38)
to have an effect on someone or something
60 **scout** (page 38)
someone whose job is to find people who have special abilities, for example in sports or entertainment, and give them a job
61 **honour** (page 38)
a prize that someone is given because they have done something important
62 **national treasure** (page 41)
something that is an important part of a country's history and culture. A *national treasure* is not allowed to leave the country.
63 **run** – *to run something* (page 41)
to control and organize something such as a business, organization or event

64 **hosted** – *to host something* (page 42)
   to arrange a special event and provide the area, equipment or services needed for it

65 **disqualified** – *to disqualify someone* (page 42)
   to not allow someone to take part in something, usually because they have done something wrong

66 **qualifying** (page 42)
   to *qualify* is to reach a particular stage of a competition by competing successfully in an earlier stage. A *qualifying match* is a match at this stage.

67 **sacked** – *to sack someone* (page 42)
   to make someone leave their job

68 **reputation** (page 42)
   the opinion that people have about how good or bad someone or something is

69 **marvel** (page 43)
   someone or something that is very surprising or impressive

70 **share** (page 44)
   one of the equal parts of a company that you can buy as a way of investing money

71 **decade** (page 44)
   a period of ten years

72 **pre-seasonal** (page 46)
   relating to the time before the season – the period of the year when a particular sport is played – begins

73 **sleeping giant** (page 47)
   used to describe a person or group of people who you think will be important and powerful in the future

74 **result** (page 49)
   success that you achieve

75 **ornamental** (page 50)
   used to make things look good

76 **charity** (page 50)
   a *charity match* is organized to raise money for charity – an organization that gives money to people who need help

77 **ought not** – *ought not to do something* (page 50)
   used for saying that something is not the right or sensible thing to do, or not the right way to behave

78 **diet** (page 53)
   the food that a person or animal usually eats

79 **pace** (page 53)
the speed at which something happens or is done

80 **EU** (page 53)
the European Union: an organization of European countries whose aim is to improve business among its members and encourage closer political connections

81 **case** (page 54)
a *legal* matter that will be decided in a court. If something is *legal*, it is allowed by the law or done according to the law.

82 **agent** (page 54)
someone whose job is to help a person by finding work for them, or to help a person or company by dealing with their business

83 **trophy** (page 56)
a large gold or silver cup or similar object that is given as a prize to the winner of a sports competition

84 **organized** – *to organize something* (page 57)
to prepare or arrange an activity or event

85 **stage** (page 57)
a certain point in time during a process or series of events

86 **knockout** (page 57)
a stage in which a player or team that loses a game leaves the competition

87 **drawn** – *to draw someone or something* (page 57)
to choose one team or person to play against another in a competition

88 **aggregate** (page 57)
the total scored in a set of games

89 **bid** – *to bid for something* (page 59)
to offer to do work or provide a service

90 **badge** (page 60)
an object with words or pictures on it. You put it on your clothes, for example to show that you support an idea or a political party

91 **tactical** (page 60)
done as part of a plan for winning something

92 **outspoken** (page 61)
an *outspoken* person states their opinion honestly, even if other people do not like it

93 **turned against** – *to turn against someone or something* (page 61)
to stop liking or supporting someone or something and start
opposing them

94 **promotion** (page 61)
a move to a higher level in a company or sport

95 **celebrity** (page 61)
a famous entertainer or sports personality

96 **temporary** (page 63)
if you do a *temporary* job, you do it for a limited period of time

97 **stability** (page 64)
a situation in which things continue without any big changes or
problems

98 **ability** (page 65)
the skill that you need in order to do something

99 **risk** (page 65)
the possibility that something bad or dangerous might happen

100 **discipline** (page 67)
the ability to control your own behaviour

101 **incident** (page 68)
something that happens that is unusual, violent or dangerous

Definitions adapted from the Macmillan Essential Dictionary © *Macmillan Publishers Limited 2003*
www.macmillandictionaries.com

Exercises

True or False?

Read the statements about the Story of Football. Write T (True) or F (False).

1	In early ball games each team had five players.	F
2	In these games the loser was killed.	
3	In China and Japan players could not touch the ball.	
4	Greek players played without clothes.	
5	The Romans played football in Britain.	
6	Football was banned in many places in England after the Romans left.	
7	In rugby you can hold the ball.	
8	Men played football in factories while they were working.	
9	The first football club in the world was in Sheffield.	
10	The Football Association was founded in 1853.	
11	There were fourteen FA rules.	
12	Goals had no crossbars or nets before 1890.	
13	Referees used whistles from 1878.	
14	The first players all wore different colour shirts.	
15	Players' shirts have always had sponsors' logos on them.	

The Early Years

Complete the gaps. Use each year in the box once.

1992	1894	1927	~~1888~~
1913	1928	1892	1887
1965	1890	1898	1891

1 The first football league started in ...._1888_........ .

2 Nets for goals were introduced in ....

3 Penalty kicks were allowed in ....

4 Games had one referee and two linesmen in ....

5 There were seventeen official rules in ....

6 The Rangers stadium was built in ....

7 The first purpose-built stadium in England opened in ....

8 The first radio commentary was in ....

9 The goalkeeper wore a different coloured shirt from ....

10 Players wore numbers on their shirts from ....

11 Another player was allowed to play if one was injured from

....

12 Names were added to players shirts in ....

People in the Story

Write a name or names next to the correct information below. You can use the names more than once.

> Stanley Matthews   Dixie Dean   Cliff Bastin   Bobby Moore
> Bobby Charlton   George Best

1 _____Bobby Charlton_____ spent most of his career playing for Manchester United.

2 _____ never got a red or yellow card.

3 _____ was born in Northern Ireland.

4 _____ was in a plane crash in Germany.

5 _____ scored sixty goals in one season.

6 _____ stopped playing football professionally when he was fifty.

7 _____ was the youngest player to win a cap.

8 _____ played in the 1966 World Cup.

9 _____ was captain of England in the 1966 World Cup.

10 _____ became famous for his lifestyle.

11 _____ joined Arsenal for two thousand pounds.

12 _____ was given an OBE by the Queen.

13 _____ earned twenty pounds a week.

14 _____ was the first footballer to be knighted.

Multiple Choice

Tick the best answer.

1 Who wanted to become the head of his country?
   - **a** Didier Drogba
   - **b** George Weah ✓
   - **c** Emmanuel Eboue

2 Which Premier League club trains young Indian people in England?
   - **a** Arsenal
   - **b** Manchester United
   - **c** West Ham

3 Which Russian club was linked to the police in the USSR?
   - **a** Spartak
   - **b** Locomotiv
   - **c** Dynamo

4 Which country did Turkey play their first international match against?
   - **a** Bulgaria
   - **b** Romania
   - **c** Croatia

5 When did the FA accept the Women's Football Association?
   - **a** in the 1970s
   - **b** in the 1980s
   - **c** in the 1990s

6 Where were ninety-six people killed?
   - **a** the Heysel Stadium
   - **b** the Hillsborough Stadium
   - **c** the Galatasaray Stadium

7 Who wants teams to have a minimum of six home players?
   - **a** Jean-Marc Bosman
   - **b** Sepp Blatter
   - **c** Michel Platini

8　Why do European teams want to be in the top four of their domestic league?

　　a　to play in the European Championship

　　b　to play in the Champions' league

　　c　to play in the World Cup

9　When were the first modern Olympic Games held?

　　a　in 1896

　　b　in 1876

　　c　in 1851

10　Who was given the award for the World's Best Football Manager twice?

　　a　Alex Ferguson

　　b　Arsene Wenger

　　c　José Mourinho

11　What is a problem for referees today?

　　a　the owners

　　b　television

　　c　the fans

12　Where do the biggest clubs have football academies?

　　a　in their own countries only

　　b　in other countries only

　　c　in their own countries and other countries

Vocabulary: Football

Complete the gaps. Use each word in the box once.

dribbles	saves	substitute	scores	coach	hat trick	banned
tackle	referee	pace	formation	~~pitch~~	spectators	penalty

1 Football is played on a .... *pitch* ....

2 The person who trains the players is called the ....

3 The person who checks the players are following the rules is the
....

4 The footballer who plays when another player cannot is the
....

5 The people who go to watch the game are ....

6 The players are arranged into a .... on the pitch.

7 When the goalkeeper stops the ball, he .... it.

8 When a player tries to get the ball from another player, it is a
....

9 When a player moves the ball with small kicks, he
.... it.

10 If something is officially not allowed, it is ....

11 When a player kicks the ball into the goal and it goes in, he
....

12 When a player scores three goals in the same match, it is a
....

13 If a game is played in a fast way, it has ....

14 If one team breaks a rule, the other team can have a
....

Vocabulary: Odd one out

Tick the word which is different.

1 Which word is NOT football clothing?
  a material ✓
  b kit
  c pads
  d strip

2 Which word is NOT a position of a player in football?
  a striker
  b defender
  c winger
  d slave

3 Which verb is NOT done in a game of football?
  a to defend
  b to trip up
  c to reject
  d to tackle

4 Which word is NOT part of a football competition?
  a group stage
  b knockout stage
  c replica
  d trophy

5 Which word is NOT a job?
  a commentator
  b opponent
  c engineer
  d manager

Vocabulary: Countries and nationalities

Complete the table with the missing words. The missing words are all in the story.

COUNTRY	NATIONALITY
Sweden	1 *Swede*
2	Greek
Mexico	3
4	Brazilian
Russia	5
Argentina	6
The Netherlands	7
8	Portuguese
9	Ghanaian
Japan	10
Spain	11
12	Turkish

Words from the Story

Match the words from the story to their meanings.

1	someone who is competing against you	D	A	discipline
2	the opinion people have about how good or bad something is		B	to retire
3	a move to a higher level in a company or sport		C	temporary
4	a very careful copy of something		D	opponent
5	to make someone leave their job		E	slave
6	the ability to control your own behaviour		F	to sack someone
7	correct in every way		G	to reject
8	something which is very, very old		H	reputation
9	a person or team who want to win the same competition		I	to influence
10	to stop working when you get old		J	replica
11	to not accept something		K	rival
12	a period of ten years		L	accurate
13	something which is for a limited period of time		M	celebrity
14	to have an effect on someone or something		N	promotion
15	a person who is not free		O	decade
16	someone who is famous		P	ancient

Grammar: *Who* or *which*?

Rewrite the two sentences to make one sentence using *who* or *which*.

Example	Zamora was a goalkeeper. He was born in 1901.
	Zamora, who was a goalkeeper, was born in 1901.

1   Alfredo di Stéfano played for Madrid. He was from Argentina.

2   Maradona's transfer fee was five million pounds. It set a new record.

3   Maradona was captain of the Argentinian team. He has now retired.

4   Pelé learnt how to play football from his father. He was called a 'national treasure'.

5   Brazil is the home of beautiful football. It has one of the largest stadiums in the world.

6   Football in the USA was popular with immigrants. It has a longer history than most people think.

7   David Beckham was signed by LA Galaxy. He increased interest in football in the USA.

Grammar: Past simple active and passive

Complete the sentences using the verbs in brackets. Use the past simple active or passive.

1 Some Englishmen _____introduced_____ (introduce) football to France.

2 FIFA _____ (start) in 1904.

3 The European Championship 1984 _____ (hold) in France.

4 Manchester United _____ (sign) Eric Cantona.

5 Football _____ (play) in Germany for the first time in 1900.

6 Jürgen Klinsmann _____ (score) forty-seven international goals.

7 Modern football _____ (bring) to Italy in the 1880s.

8 Juventus _____ (found) in 1897.

9 Paulo Rossi _____ (give) the Golden Boot Award.

10 Gianfranco Zola _____ (name) best ever Chelsea player in 2003.

11 Frank Rijkaard _____ (manage) the Dutch national team.

12 Marco van Basten's career _____ (begin) in 1981.

13 In 1995, his career _____ (end) by an injury.

14 Eusébio _____ (be) the first winner of the European Golden Boot.

Macmillan
Readers

www.macmillanenglish.com/readers

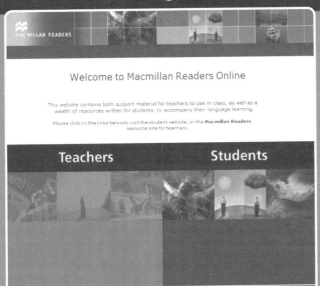

Welcome to Macmillan Readers Online

This website contains both support material for teachers to use in class, as well as a wealth of resources written for students, to accompany their language learning.

Please click on the links below to visit the student website, or the **Macmillan Readers** resource site for teachers.

Teachers   **Students**

MACMILLAN   © Copyright Macmillan Publishers 2007 Terms & Conditions

- **Students' section** featuring *The Book Corner Club,* for those students who want to study Readers in a book club. It also features tips for creative writing and essays, a level test, webquests and URLs for further reading, articles, interviews with authors, audio, poetry and author biography worksheets
- **Teachers' section** with expanded collection of free support material including worksheets, answer keys, sample chapters, sample audio, webquests, author data sheets and the *Using Graded Readers in the Classroom* guide

MACMILLAN READERS

Published by Macmillan Heinemann ELT
Between Towns Road, Oxford OX4 3PP
A division of Macmillan Publishers Limited
Companies and representatives throughout the world
Heinemann is the registered trademark of Pearson Education, used under licence.

ISBN 978–0–2304–0049–8
ISBN 978–0–2304–0050–4 (with CD edition)

First published 2010
Text © Macmillan Publishers Limited 2010
Design and illustration © Macmillan Publishers Limited 2010
This version first published 2010

Illustrated by John Dillow
Cover photograph by Alamy / vario images GmbH & Co.KG

The authors and publishers would like to thank the following for
permission to reproduce their photographic material: **Alamy** / Lordprice
Collection p11; **Corbis** / Mike Finn-Kelcey/ Reuters p48, Corbis / Stephen
Hird/ Reuters p72; **Getty Images** / pp27, 51, 59, 64, Getty Images / Bob
Thomas p39; **Mary Evans Picture Library** / p16; **Press Association
Images** / Thomas Eisenhuth p43; **The Art Archive** / Museo Nazionale
Terme Rome / Gianni Dagli Orti p8.

Printed and bound in Thailand

without CD edition
2012 2011 2010
7   6   5   4   3

with CD edition
2012 2011 2010
6   5   4   3   2